Sail Away The Plenty

Sail Away The Plenty

Poems

Kathleen M. McCann

Cover layout: Shay Culligan
Cover artist: Jean Donohue
Cover painting: Vincent Crotty
Author photograph: Cindy Lou Pelaquin

ISBN: 978-1-950462-22-3

Kelsay Books Inc.

kelsaybooks.com

502 S 1040 E, A119
American Fork, Utah 84003

Acknowledgments

Blackbird: "Sea Store,"

Crannog: "Annie Moore"

The Dalhousie Review: "Stitch In The Stocking"

Palo Alto Review: "American Wake," "Pastoral Ireland"

Rhino: "Black '47"

The Threepenny Review: "Bone Dust"

Poetry Ireland Review: "Crossing to England for Harvest Work"

Contents

II The Far Shore

III The Future's Pronouncement

Ireland
That ragged
leaking raft held
between sea and sea.

—Richard Ryan

I

Better the Fields

Botanical Gardens, Dublin, September 1845

Blight is a capricious disease.
—Stephen Campbell

Trial pots of potato plants
curl at the edges, blacken:
prognosis for the *Evening Post:*
   —*phytophthora infestans*—
blight. Appearances earlier in England,
and the Continent.
By October, widespread reports
of rot, waste of crop: Waterford,
Antrim, Clare and Monaghan,
decimated parts of the west.
In the form of a fungus, misery
with murderous repercussions: typhus,
dysentery, *bloody flux,* and ship fever
when the fleeing starts.
Death, under a hillside's wind,
ship's sail.
Assistance for the tiny towns:
relief centers, work projects,
soup kitchens, evangelicals,
base camp for the brave
or foolish.
Leave it to the historians to parse
the politics, second-guess history.
It takes all the strength one can gather
to stand and look over history's fields.
Kilkee, whose churchyards
opened up
trenches for the bodies
slid from hinge-based reusable coffins,
covered with quicklime.

Black '47

The stench of rotting potatoes wafted throughout Ireland.
                                        —Stephen Campbell

When the wind blew the millions
of spores, the tiny seed-like
particles of destruction,
the air took them.
Fetch and carry;
history of the world.
Gone, all trace of white
or purple flower.
The berries erased
in the rot and squelch of spud.

Summer Hunger

Give the spuds to the ground
in April and May; *lazy beds,*
seeds set, prodded and prayed
over. Patience,
the poor's parish.

Set the chin for autumn.
Lift the spuds to the layered
straw pits covered with earth
to keep until June,
no longer.

The long sleeve…four
to five;
hunger clots the gut.
Barley and oats
only: *meal months.*

Fever Sheds

After death the lice would leave the cooling body
and transfer to anyone nearby.
—Stephen Campbell

Too small for the numbers pouring in,
workhouse hospitals kept sickness
shut up tight, death's tin drum tickling
the ear.
No space to keep sick
from well, nothing to do
but put up *fever sheds,*
promise of help.
The going
and coming of death's
long sordid tide.
Everyone
afraid to touch.
Better to light up sheds
blue and blazing,
rotting corpses inside.

The Clearances

*The famine and the agricultural depression of 1849-52 spelled the
extinction of middlemen's position as intermediate landlords. They
were ground into dust between the upper and nether millstones.*
                                        —James S. Donnelly, Jr.

Landlords long sought to bypass middlemen,
get back to rents taken directly from smallholders.
Collect, or be dispossessed by creditors,
no choice for the landlords who let go
the middleman, cut off any further sublets.
Smallholders as well faced dispossession;
a desperate timeout in the workhouse
could return a house unroofed.
Drastic measure, the wide sweep of clearances
begun in 1846, continued into the next year
with the tolling of a new word dinging
the air, *extermination,* removal
in full force.
The quarter-acre clause, starvation, rampant
disease, all loosened the smallholder's grip;
rent in arrears, a growing poor tax,
money pouch cinched sooner
and sooner, sent landlords for the brawn.

The smallholder's toppling stool: surrender
to the workhouse, emigrate,
beg at the roadsides.
A landlord, feet up and head back
thinks: cheaper to assist with emigration
than support the workhouse,
feed and clothe, though poorly,
a diminishment of bodies.
The tenant's choice: a flip
of a coin so thin

there is no other side.
Emigrate, board a coffin ship
and sail…Australia, Canada, America,
or stay home, unable to meet the rent,
a hair's breadth from the hammer,
MP's crowbar brigade come to
   —never with any left inside—
level the cabin.

Timber and Thatch

Tenants frequently unroofed their own cabins as part of a voluntary surrender in which they were graciously allowed to take away the timber and thatch of their former dwellings.

—James Donnelly, Jr.

How much longer can the cottiers
and tenants-at-will hold the requisite
quarter-acre, avoid the MPs
with their crowbar brigade's
thirst to *tumble* the cottage?
The workhouse
waits. Not for you
or yours, pride's burn
in the chest.
Better the fields,
rag-tag wind,
the roadside
at which
to beg,
die.

A Tax on Every Window

Pauper, poor folk, potato
pickers, any derisive term
would do for those
who worked the land
they did not own.
Sir Robert Goore-Booth, Anglo-
Irish landowner kept
a tight belt, rents on time
or the gutter, brush-off
and get up, or die there.
Pity the one who'd try to improve
his wet square, puny plot,
rents rose with the effort: a tax
on every window, as well
the chimney.
Go without, straight-back
of the poor, the proud;
fill the windows with straw,
forego a hint of sky.
The Sir's eyes set on eight hundred acres,
Ballygilgan, North Sligo land;
a handshake across Lord Lorton's table,
'The Seven Carrons' to him.

One hundred some families…
rents paid, bills squared,
kiss off.
The Sir's cattle will put down their tongues
right there.
For 800 acres, one hundred poor souls
will disappear, sure as the historian's
footnote; passage stamped for the *Pomano*,
sail set on a watery grave,

not America.
No room now for those who dared
remain, cottages so close to the Sir and his lady;
she, no fan of the turf smoke.
Heave ho to the dwellings! Demolish
the roofs and throw down the walls.
Dear God, get out before
the battering ram! Never mind

the children, scuttling underfoot,
women on the run reaching for a pot
or a pan, hugging a door frame.
Remember too the old woman who went
to her knees for mercy and rose
with a curse:
　　　　the Gore-Booths will melt from the face of the earth.

Stirabout

In the short term, soup was supposed to bring salvation.
       —James Donnelly, Jr.

  1 pound of meal or flour.
  Add water swelling to a ration
  weighing 3 to 5 pounds.

Serve with a biscuit or piece of bread
to all over nine years of age. For those
under age, halve the biscuit, bread.
Mind the consistency. Too liquidy,
danger of diarrhea in the warm weather;
too thick, understood.
Ladle the line,

but make it last.

One Potato, Two Potato

One potato, two potato, three potato, four,
five potato, six potato, seven potato, more.

No potato, no potato, no potato, more,
down the lane and up the lane the coffins crowd the door.

In the circle, out the circle, oh, the Brits stand high,
see the Micks—Jig-etee-jigging,—all their spuds gone by.

Queuing Up for the Soup

Coffinless,
to horse-drawn carts,
all over Ireland
the dead go out
the door.
Those left
lower the latch,
turn back to food
as reverie, sickness
the plenty.
Some take to the soup line,
order and stamp,
inching; heads hung
to bury a horizon
of others.
Tin cups loose
at the side
might as well fall through
fingertips; lips mutter,
                    the hell with it.

Bone Dust

Done because we are one too menny.
—Thomas Hardy

The heart could break
if not for the morning
waiting at the door, press
of expectant mouths.
Workhouse inmates: men,
women and children,
sledge hammer stones into gravel,
crush animal bone into powder
for fertilizer,
until the guards discover them
eating the bone dust.

Pig in the Parlor

The dung heap was a symbol of wealth, not poverty.
　　　　　　　　　　—Stephen Campbell

won't curl by the hearth,
rise and stretch a long
sleepy dog's welcome,
familiar as an old song.

Kit and caboodle, part
and parcel of domestic space;
public as well, and the dung heap's size,
by the side of the house, counts.

Measure the heap, measure
the wealth. Foraging pigs, fat
inside and out, slop up spuds
and eliminate. That's that.

Famine Scene in Old Chapel Lane, Skibbereen, Co. Cork

from *The Illustrated London News,* November 13, 1847

A lane as narrow
as teeth.
Bent figures cluster
in doorways, talk
taken outside.
Two shrouded women kneel
beside an empty lorry,
another upturned onto hay.
Chimneys poke a woozy sky
under salt and pepper slant.
The lane disappears uphill
where the artist's hand is heavy.
Churlish, foreboding strokes,
vicious collection, full sea bearing down.

An Gorta Mór

The streets are gray
where death's chalky hand
rubs the days. Remains
throughout the evenings' dank hours, barest rooms,
for the weakest.

Those shut away
from the roadsides, feckless fields,
must summon what strength
and let go. Loose the soul,
birdsong, faint and flown already beyond.

Poteen

More heft tonight,
put the buttermilk
by.
To hell with it all.
Quiet the ruckus.
Raise the yeasty jug.

Kilrush Union Clearances

As long as the habere was in force, every occupier
of the lands could be removed at an hour's notice.
Captain Arthur Kennedy, Poor Law official

Two thousand seven-hundred families,
evicted. Deep-throated word rising to test
its mettle, stolid strength pitting the powerless.
First to go, the landless labourers doubling
as fishermen, slipping off the long coast,
tackle let for food.
Offers to help, money or shelter,
meant exemption from the *hanging gale,*
a half-year's rent allowed to stand in arrears.
Haberes, possession decrees, did quick work,
scattered Ireland's luckless seed. *Indolent*
men booted with their women and children
bumped against one another in bog holes,
roadside ditches, hillside hovels—*scalpins*—
roofed with thatch from a *tumbled* cottage.
Face to walled earth, the dark and deep of stalled time.
Hear the poor law officer's strident voice
shouting down the murderous convictions.
Standing on the back of a haywagon, his
young daughter—*her daily occupation*—
holds out clothes to the *wretched* children.

Outdoor Relief

Laissez-faire, Britain's brittle-boned policy
of giving little, gave enough to amend
the 1838 Poor Laws, promote Outdoor Relief.
Outdoor Relief, families could stay at home,
spared the workhouse humiliation—
separation from one another, forced eating in
silence, forbidden to leave.
Home, shame's bloom on the face
of men queuing up at the state's teat,
taking day-labor from the Board of Works;
stirabout: two-thirds Indian meal/one-third rice/
tepid water from the soup kitchen.
Little of nothing
from a mousy bowl.
Filmy-mirage: —lush field in the distance—
fools the mind and body's lack of plenty.

Buttermilk and the Bleaching Green

Linen, the country's finest fabric,
brought to boil in a solution of water
and ashes, seaweed, or fermented bran,
rinsed, then spread on the bleached-green
grass. Aired, steeped
in buttermilk, rinsed
and dried,
steeped again.
Repetition,
wisdom's know-how.
Linen, cloth of kings, championed
choice the Irish clutched, flax
sprung to full effect when wool
and woolen cloth saw curtailment,
let go but little for England and Wales,
per order of England's Parliament Act, 1699.
Cannot keep the resilient down.
Flax, small seed from the grass family,
offered its brown for crushing,
again for threshing.
Stalks immersed, held under by stone
in the lint holes—flax dams—the poorer
portions decay and slough off.
With time, the stalks are pulled
from the holes and left to dry,
a putrid stink.
Retting next for the bound
and bundled flax, breakdown of flax stalk
and necessary period for rotting,
fermentation before the scutch mill's
pulverization, separation of the sought
after fiber from wood and pulp

underneath toothed rollers, a step
away from the wooden paddle,
water wheel's last beating.
Waged war,
solo operators who sit at each paddle,
endure.
Endurance, Irish history's long
arm of it back to 1260: Battle of Downpatrick,
mail clad Normans defeat Brian O' Neill's army,
dressed in linen.

Mass in a Connemara Cabin

—Aloysius O'Kelly, 1883

Kindly priest, tall and straight
as a stick, soft set to his face.
Nothing hard about him.
From underneath his pristine
chasuble, the right hand rises.
Maybe pity prompts the hand its rise
—beyond bare cupboards—
for a blessing, benediction
in the cabin's close air.
Home-bound parishioners,
poor as the day is long,
bow their heads
on knees brought numb by dirt.
The body's frailties…gurgle
and roil of empty bellies
brings shame to the face.

Spailpin

If we had potatoes and turf, we would have life on our rear ends.
                    —an old Irish Traditional song

Conacre's bull, humping potatoes
past your mouth
for rent.
Landless labourer,
itinerancy lures you
for as little as eight
pence to a shilling.
Winding along
down the Shannon's
verdant banks, lush
Munster, Leinster, figuring
for a *strong farm,* if *measure*
be made at the *hiring fair,*
deeming you fit
for the *fookin'* spuds.
Hoboing Ireland's west coast,
dreaming food for the family.
Full bellies the push.

Ribbonmen

Ragtag motley crew
fed old resentments.
And new, fresh in the cheek,
canker the tongue bothers.

Rambling rabblers, shit
stirrers stroking hurts,
nib-nudging folks
for a row.

What good comes
of doing nothing,
when nothing is all
that's come?

* *Ribbonism was an organized form of agrarian and sometimes sectarian violence.*

The White House

There were six teams of master masons, each team consisting of ten men,
some of whom heaved the stone into shape in Slieve Bawn, some doing the
designs on the stone, some laying the stone…
                    —an anonymous descendant of one of the workers

And so on…languid phrase,
conjures a meandering river.
So forth…stones lifted and hauled
from nearby Sieve Bawn by men
bending to mind-splitting work,
spiritless work fit to crush, spill
the plenty right out of a man.
Full bellies for the men who set a palatial
home fast and firm for Thomas Mahon,
fairs and markets below.
Nothing too good for Mahon's Strokestown,
a show-stopping 147-foot-wide main street
modeled after the Ringstrasse in Vienna;
a linen trade with bleached cloth to rival
the west's finest. Narrowness,
none here.
Nor the White House with its three-decade completion,
two hundred workmen: carpenters, artisans, joiners,
apprentice understudies, fetchers and runners. Even mules,
mixing and turning the dry mortar, grunt work,
straining and pulling the days through the days.
Mahon's White House, remarked on by all who passed:
Arthur Young, the English travel writer arriving in August, 1776,
marveled at the trees—*oak, English and French elm, beech, maple,*
spruce, Scotch and silver, fur, larch, all with their bright and
beautiful bark—*And so on.*
Compliments to the Big House,
locals name for landed gentries' residencies.

Privileged place
built on the backs of those who would starve
soon enough,
dropping in ditches and fields,
grass stained mouths, a last
grasp at food.

Pastoral Ireland

Tourists' draw: sheep nibbling grass
in the high hills, spray painted
colors—blue, green,
ungodly orange.
Toy cottages, a curl of smoke
threading a mellow sky, ubiquitous
border collie yipping in the open air,
the sea, sturdy-study of tranquility,
poured to a well-hewn frame
of fine and rich mahogany.
Tranquility sells.
This is not *The Cabin at Doogh,*
County Mayo, Fairbolt's finely-wrought
sketch of misery, cabins like beehives,
charcoaled hump-backed black hills,
sky, chalk-white nothing.
Ten thousand lie in the Famine graveyard
of Abbeystrewery.
A community of souls, unidentified,
slid from earth to earth
in serviceable bottom-hinged coffins
that drop, double back for more.

Crossing to England for Harvest Work

There were those who were brought over as ballast, 'huddled like pigs,' others were landed secretly on the Welsh coast before the vessels reached port and dropped by night, in the mud...
　　　　　　　　　　　　　　—Cecil Woodham-Smith

Fever, exhaustion, hunger's
hitch conjures an urge to
sink, give in
to the mud's seductive
suck and pull; drop
to the knees,
lower the head
and let go.
Let the mind blow out;
bright breath, body's
bee, float away.
Effortless, nonchalant
wave of the hand,
a grand day.

Sail Away the Plenty, 1847

Peas, beans, rabbits, salmon, honey—
Ireland to England, four thousand trips.
Stiffest of sails, four thousand ships
sail away the plenty.

American Wake

So many of the best go.
  —Old Irish lament

Dogs, donkeys, horses, wild
birds, nuts, berries, dandelions,
the occasional herb, eat them all.
Boil away the meager cabbage
and turnips, it won't keep them,
the older ones straightening by the hedge,
having turned the front latch and stepped beyond
a mother's wet eyes and quivering lips,
the young ones in the corner, sleepy-eyed.
At the church a solemn priest steps into
the road for a blessing before the boat –
    God be with ya', my sons and daughters,
        God be with ya'.

II

The Far Shore

The Far Shore

Full up, September 7, 1849,
the brig St. John: nine crew,
a hundred or more passengers,
two hundred tons—persons, parcel, wood.
Timber of ship and sail, pushing out
from Galway Bay, air thick
with the travelers' anxiety.
Cast-offs, neither fickle
nor free.
Caps set for the far shore.
Boston or bust.

Stitch in the Stocking

A wife never let her man go to sea
without threading her singular stitch,
clear and clean as his name,
through the wool's burly blur.

A woman with her man gone to danger
lives in the crease of terror's hardened nights;
the bed, only a box for bee-hived nerves,
anxiety's metered melt serving time.

Fire low, the children asleep....
A thousand pardons for the one who must come,
cupping the awful burden of wet wool
to firelight, a widow's face.

Sea Store

Emigrants were given a sea-store consisting of tea, coffee, sugar, rice, oatmeal, dried fish and vinegar.

—Steven Campbell

Sugar and salt for the palette,
given in exchange for home:
church bell's toll
above the familiar; get away
spot for lovers,
loners.
Emigrate, or starve.
Choice, a coin hammered to tree's cross,
tarnished relic rusting in woods' ruin,
no face for the future.

Wreck of the Brig St. John, Cohasset, Massachusetts October 7, 1849

Flimsy fodder, ballast,
beam, shiftless shapes
of shingle and shard, mica
to the merciless wind.
Bystanders cannot work their eyes
beyond the hellish waves, pinpoint
those screaming, real
or imagined.

O, to be of use!
Not hand wringing in the wet air,
sighs slipping past tight

throats, grit teeth.
Tragedy, consummate narrative.
Nothing to do
but unleash the tongue
to this murderous evening.

From the Sea Room

Elizabeth Lathop offers help
worthy of an age far beyond
her own.
A brother's sudden intake of breath
sends her gaze seaward
to draw, within minutes,
a verbal image that brings
her father's professional appraisal:
    There is difficulty there,
prompting his rise from a chair
to run for the lifeboat crew
putting in at Whitehead.
Overwrought, nineteen-year-old Elizabeth
leaps the wide-pine floors
for the shoreline
where her brother and fellow
townspeople queue up
to save, God's mercy,
any left alive.

A Parcel

Out of the swell
and gnarl of a wild surf
the sea gives.

Mr. Lathop opens his arms
to *a parcel of clothing*
and nets the full-throated

cry of an infant.
Cupped to his chest
all the way in, clasped

in trembling hands.

Catherine Flanagan, Age Twenty

I will live to be ninety-two,
thrive in New England's seaside.
All my life, a townie.

I will mark my days
by the sky's whimsy,
the sweet slow turn to season.

I will marry,
but not young, wisdom
the rudder of my life.

Ruinous roil
of the sea....
Death, pass by.

Thoreau's Journal

Headed for Cape Cod when the tragedy struck,
he and his traveling companion turned
to take the south shore's back roads:
> *We met several hay-riggings and farm-wagons*
> *each loaded with three large, rough deal boxes.*
> *We did not need to ask what was in them.*

A woman had emigrated from Ireland
on an earlier ship:
> *She had left her infant behind for her sister to bring*
> *and came and looked into these boxes, and saw in one*
> *her child in her sister's arms, as if the sister had meant*
> *to be found thus; and within three days after, the mother*
> *died from the effect of the sight.*

Captain of his fate, his conscience,
concise Concordian, nothing to do
but look on,
and write.
Bring the eye of the incident
to bear, for those
who had the stomach.
Whole families, like the Sweeneys
from Galway, husband and wife, nine
children, bodies mangled and mauled by the rocks,
all but Sally, perhaps with the bitterest irony
befitting a mother:
> *presenting features that were calm*
> *and placid, as if she were enjoying*
> *a quiet and pleasant slumber.*

Bodies thrown to the shore's rocks,
sucked again and again into
the foam's brick of backwash.
By nightfall, forty-six bodies…

coffined on the beach, prayed and watched over,
buried under Tuesday's clear air.
Staying to watch the funeral procession,
Thoreau pencils to his journal:
> *On the whole, it was not so impressive a scene as I might*
> *have expected. The sight of one body affects us deeply*
> *but the sight of so many bodies blunted the sensibilities.*
You who could tremble in a moment
of transcendence, touched to the quick
crossing Concord's common,
tremble again.
Disappointment,
this time.

Found Poem: List of Famine Ships that Advertised in and Serviced Galway, 1845-1850

Abbotsford	Fanny	Minerva
Albion	Francis-Watte	Nancy
Alice	GEM	Napoleon
Agimou	G.W.Brinkerhoff	Ohip
Barbara	G.W. Lawrence	Pacific
Bethel	Haidee	Pageant
Cambyses	Helena	Plant
Carctacus	Henderson	Preciosa
Caroline	H. Mellon	Rebecca
Cashmere	IHN John	Redwing
Celeste	Irvine	Sarah Milledge
C.H. Appelton	John Begg	Seabird
Charlotte	John Clifford	St. John
Clarence	Josephine	Tassie
Clytha	Joshua Carroll	Thalia
Coldstream	Kate	The Asia
Commence	Laing	The Lucullus
Carrib	Lelia	The Medora
Cremona	Linden	Thetis
Cushlamachree	Lively	Thomas Baker
Daniel	Lord Fitzgerald	Valhalla
David	Lord Fitzroy	Viceroy
Delphin	Lyna	Victoria
Doctor Kneises	Malvina	Wakefield
Downes	Manchester	Walkella
Eliza Ann	Margaret Milne	William Kerry
Elizabeth Hughes	Maria	Young Queen
Emma Prescott	Maine Plant	
Emmeline	Martha	

Longing

For the ego, its overbearing pose,
lamb's wool lullaby, to sock it away.

For the body, sinew and nerves, a doze
and drift; dream's glass sea, mainstay.

For the evening, a mossy close,
slow sweet slip of day.

III

The Future's Pronouncement

Famine

A word without
corners. No
flint nor force
to fling.

Instead, a wafer-
thin cry running
hills, barren fields,
the sea's mute stay.

Helloooo….
Chambered-echo
of breath
let go…let go.

The Old Country

A history of gray,
taut nerves, mistrust
on the mind.

Too little
always, leaves
one timid or

angry. Humor's gold
coin, the wry joke
with sting.

All of Ireland Goes Begging

—for Andrea Mori

Riff the pipes
hard. Play

that tin whistle
good night.

Make the air
sing.

Annie Moore

What was it like, the final walk out
over the fields, kissing your favorite
lamb on the head, last look
before a hand reluctantly lifts
to wave away home?
Twelve days minding the thump and drone of sea,
settled into steerage with your underling brothers,
eleven year-old Anthony, seven year-old Philip.
Thursday evening, Christmas Eve, the S.S. Nevada's
one hundred and forty-eight passengers make land;
America wakes you to the new year, your
fifteenth birthday. Happy Birthday, Annie,
infamous traveler, bronzed both in the going
and coming: County Cork – Ellis Island, New York.
One hand raised to hold the hat in place,
valise in the other, pressed firm against
a blowsy, full skirt, three-quarter jacket
closed tight, every button snug for travel.
Eyes firm and fast, the future's pronouncement.

A Child's Game

The wonder ball goes round and round, to pass it quickly you are bound...

Where does grief get off
hauling hackneyed phrases
over the back like sailors' gear?

Grief, shunted hot potato
shuffled off...*ooh,*
sting to the fingertips.

Grief, world's first
wonder ball, passed
and passed

and passed.

Reading An Irish Anthology On Vacation

Kavanagh's candle is lit for Maguire,
champion of Ireland's famished people;
the entire church body, staunch believers
in ritual's balm, aglow for him.
I'll toggle my own switch
when I get home, a dollar in the box,
a fire-proofed prayer to the Blessed Virgin,
my mother's assurance, life long comfort:
    Holy Mary, Mother of God,
    Blessed is the fruit of thy womb, Jesus.
How many nights, mumbling again the beads;
Lady's Sodality, no matter the weather.
Faith for her was no fickle find. Always
Mary, mother of God....

I'll go during the week when no one's there.
Midweek's let down, over-the-hump Wednesday.
No fidgety children, cell phones, sharp coughs,
nor rustling robed priest tapping his mic,
boring down on the exegetic bone.

Passing of the peace, not necessary.
One red candle
for a mother who loved
her Mary.

Penance

Climbing the stairs each early evening
up over the worn wood, creak and cracks
of home,
would dreams take you back to the farm's edge,
fields rife with potato and turf,
Clifden's rimmed rocks, rooks' hammered ring
and rise in the air, Sky Road's lovely
long-ranged views?

Here, in Boston's backyard,
you lived long past the years' poor trade:
fifteen-year-old Irish girl
come over, turned
grandmother of three,
boarder in the grown daughter's home,
door stop in the family dynamic.

Away and away you crept those nights
with your bad eyes and bum joints,
knees to hard wood under the hall's thin light.
Mouth full of penance for getting this far,
stumbling upward, masturbatory whispers…
    Jesus, Mary, and Joseph—stabled three.
Nightcap for the pain, the years,
the family below.

Ireland

Pity the slack impoverished.
Already, sons and daughters,
goods, move out beyond
the bump and groan of port.
Sail away the plenty.

Patience, Ireland's
backbone and breath.
In and out, the wearied chest
rose and fell, refused death.
Sail away the plenty.

Backward glance, years
hence, one will know
the source,
the plenty.

About the Author

Kathleen McCann lives in Weymouth, Massachusetts and has been writing poetry for over forty years. She has two chapbooks: *The Small Hours,* and *The Sea's Rosary* in print and two full-length collections: *A Roof Gone To Sky,* and *Barn Sour.* Her poems have been published in many magazines to include: *Threepenny Review; Poetry East; Sonoma Mandala Poetry Review; The Texas Review; Interim; The Comstock Review; American Writing; Borderlands;* and *The Midwest Quarterly.* One of her poems, *Lone Egret,* was selected by Ted Kooser for his syndicated newspaper column: *American Life in Poetry.* Kate is bivocational. In addition to being a poet, she serves in pastoral ministry for the United Church of Christ.

www.ingramcontent.com/pod-product-compliance
Lightning Source LLC
LaVergne TN
LVHW041309080426
835510LV00009B/914